References

King James Bible 1960

I Know
Kingdom Readers for Beginners

Author/Illustrated by Ana Salinas

Be

Be still,

Be still, and

Be still, and know

Be still, and know that

Be still, and know that
I

Be still, and know that
I am

Be still, and know that
I am God.

Psalm 46:10

The End

www.ingramcontent.com/pod-product-compliance
Lightning Source LLC
Chambersburg PA
CBHW042342300426
44109CB00048B/2727